SUSAN B. ANTHONY

Alexandra Wallner

Holiday House / New York

Library of Congress Cataloging-in-Publication Data
Wallner, Alexandra.
Susan B. Anthony / by Alexandra Wallner. — 1st ed.
p. cm.
ISBN 978-0-8234-1953-1 (hardcover)
1. Anthony, Susan B. (Susan Brownell), 1820-1906—Juvenile literature. 2. Suffragists—United States—Biography—Juvenile literature.
3. Feminists—United States—Biography—Juvenile literature. 4. Women's rights—United States—Juvenile literature. I. Title.
HQ1413.A55W35 2011
324.6'23092—dc22
[B]
2009017815

To the many wonderful women I have known who have brought
about change, both great and small, I dedicate this book.
—*Alexandra Wallner*

"Cautious, careful people never can bring about a reform."
—*Susan B. Anthony*

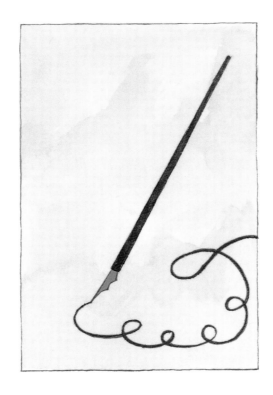

Susan Brownell Anthony was born on February 15, 1820, in Adams, Massachusetts. She was raised with six sisters and brothers by loving but strict parents who did not want their children to play with toys and games, sing songs, or paint pictures. For fun, Susan would watch a colony of ants, play in fields of wildflowers, catch snowflakes, or watch sunsets from the mountain behind her family's house.

Like most girls at that time, Susan and her sisters cooked, sewed, quilted, cleaned, and did other household chores. But the girls of Susan's family were luckier than most. Unlike many parents, Susan's wanted their daughters as well as their sons to have an education. By the time she was four, Susan had already learned to read from her grandfather.

When she was older, Susan was sent to a district school. One day she came home upset because her male instructor wouldn't teach her math. Many people believed that certain school subjects were too hard for a girl's brain. So her father, who owned a mill, started his own school for workers' children where both the boys and the girls would learn the same subjects.

Susan's father hired a young teacher named Mary Perkins, who had graduated from a good girls' school. Susan admired Mary because she was educated and earning her own living.

Susan's father was fair. But Susan found that even he was not fair all the time.

At her father's mill, Susan took over the job of a girl worker who was sick for two weeks. She earned three dollars, although the men were getting more money for doing the same jobs. She suggested to her father that he promote a girl who worked with her because she knew more about the job than her male boss. But her father said that "it would never do to have a woman overseer in the mill."

After Susan learned all she could at the factory school, she asked her father to send her to a girls' school, which he did. Now she was getting a better education, but sadly she had to leave school after just a year because of family money problems.

When she was eighteen, Susan had to decide what to do next. At the time there were only two ways for a young woman to live. Either she got married or she got a job teaching. Susan chose to be independent and rely on herself.

She got a job at a school for girls. She was worried, though, that she didn't know enough about different subjects to be a good teacher. But she soon discovered that she was still ahead of her students. Like most girls' educations, her students' had been very poor.

After a few years, even though her students liked her, she got tired of teaching because it was not a challenge anymore. But what other work could she do?

She believed that there were many things wrong with laws at that time. Women were not treated as the equals of men. They could not get a good education, own property, get equal pay, or vote, which is called "women's suffrage." There was slavery and lack of education for African Americans. She thought drinking a lot of alcohol was wrong, which is called "temperance." Susan decided to become a voice for change. These issues would be her new challenges.

Instead of teaching just a few, she would speak to many. Maybe the people who listened to her would urge lawmakers to change unfair laws. When Susan was twenty-eight, she left her safe teaching job to start an uncertain career battling for reform. It would make her unpopular, because people were not used to women speaking in public.

She used money she had saved from teaching to travel to many towns, often in winter when people were so bored they would come to any meeting and even pay money just for something to do. She did all the work herself, finding her own hotel and lecture hall and arriving early to light the room.

Sometimes people came to her speeches and made fun of her. They shouted while she was talking, threw rotten eggs at her, even threatened her with knives and pistols. In spite of these hardships, and although she was alone, she continued working for her causes.

Then Susan met Elizabeth Cady Stanton, who had organized the first convention to champion women's rights. They soon became good friends. Now Susan had someone who shared her ideas. They helped each other organize meetings and write about women's voting rights. Although Susan traveled and Mrs. Stanton usually stayed home to raise her family, Susan said, "We did better work together than either could alone."

Once Susan went to a teachers' convention in Binghamton, New York. Most of the five hundred teachers present were women who got less pay than men for the same jobs. She listened for some praise for the women teachers from the men, but there was none. Even sadder, she discovered that the women teachers did not expect any.

Some of the women who were for reform cut their hair and wore "bloomer dresses," which were shorter and easier to move in. Mrs. Stanton wore one, and finally, Susan did too.

One day when Susan came out of a post office in New York City wearing a bloomer dress, some men and boys laughed at her. They shouted and made faces. Soon she gave up wearing it. She believed that people should listen to what she had to say, not watch what she was wearing.

At a convention of men who were for temperance, Susan was not allowed to speak but told to "listen and learn" because she was a woman. She was so angry that she started a women's organization in which she and other women were able to speak freely. That was the first of many organizations she started.

During another convention, Susan organized volunteers to gather signatures on a petition to change some laws. The new laws would allow married women to own property and to vote. Although the volunteers gathered ten thousand signatures and presented the petition to lawmakers, the laws were not changed. This only made Susan more determined. She wanted "the new true woman," as she called her, to be the center of her own life.

Susan had been one voice among many that had spoken against slavery. After the Civil War, when slavery was officially abolished in the United States, Susan and Mrs. Stanton started a magazine called *The Revolution,* which pushed for the right of women and freed slaves to vote.

Then the Fifteenth Amendment was passed, giving African American men the right to vote. Women still could not cast a ballot. Susan had worked hard on many reform causes for twenty-two years, but this action made her focus. Now she would fight only for "the cause": women's suffrage.

Susan received a notice from the Internal Revenue Service saying that since *The Revolution* had earned money, taxes were owed. She wrote a letter to the government saying this was unfair. If she did not have the right to vote, why was she expected to pay taxes?

The picture above is painted from a print by Currier and Ives, *The Age of Brass or the Triumph of Women's Rights*. It shows how most men and some women felt about Susan's cause. Susan is the second from the right in the picture.

Susan continued to go to more conventions and gave more speeches. It seemed as if the law would never change. But Susan continued the battle. She said, "I am . . . in an unpopular cause and must be content to row upstream." By her fiftieth birthday she was known as the most loved and hated woman in America.

Many women who had worked with her got discouraged and quit to get married. But marriage had never interested her. A few years later she wrote, "I never felt I could give up my life of freedom to become a man's housekeeper. When I was young, if a girl married poor, she became a housekeeper and a drudge. If she married wealth she became a pet and a doll. Just think, had I married at twenty, I would have been a drudge or a doll for fifty-five years. Think of it!"

Susan argued that the Fourteenth Amendment stated that "all persons born or naturalized in the United States" could vote. It didn't say women *couldn't* vote. So she convinced fifty other women to register and vote. Susan was arrested for voting and had to stand trial. She was found guilty and ordered to pay a fine, but she never did. The trial, however, worked for her and made her and "the cause" even more famous.

Susan's battle was a long one; and even while she was fighting it, she did not believe that women would have the right to vote in her lifetime. Susan and Mrs. Stanton worked for years on a series of books called The History of Woman Suffrage to tell their story to the future women who would continue the fight.

When she was in her sixties, Susan traveled to Europe to lecture. At home, she began turning over "the cause" to younger women. Still, all decisions passed by their leader, Susan, who was by now known as the General.

Susan died on March 13, 1906, after fifty-eight years of fighting for reform. She never had the right to vote.

But her story was not finished. Those who had continued Susan's battle fought on; and in 1920, fourteen years after Susan's death, Congress voted to pass the Nineteenth Amendment to the U.S. Constitution. It gives women citizens over the age of twenty-one the right to vote. It is also called the Susan B. Anthony amendment.

In her last public speech, Susan had said, "Failure is impossible." And for Susan, it was.

TIMELINE

1820 Susan is born February 15 in Adams, Massachusetts.

1849 Susan quits teaching and begins reform work. Attends her first temperance convention.

1851 Susan meets Elizabeth Cady Stanton.

1852 Susan founds the Woman's State Temperance Society.

1861–1865 The Civil War.

1862 The Emancipation Proclamation is issued.

1865 The Thirteenth Amendment, which abolishes slavery, is ratified.

1868 Susan and Mrs. Stanton start their magazine, *The Revolution*.

1868 and 1870 Congress ratifies the Fourteenth and Fifteenth Amendments, giving citizens the right to vote no matter what race or color they are, even if they were once a slave. Since women have few rights at this time, it is taken for granted this means only men.

1870 *The Revolution*, which is losing money, is given to others to run.

1872 Susan and other women register and vote. Susan is arrested for it.

1881 The first volume of The History of Woman Suffrage is published.

1902 Mrs. Stanton dies.

1906 Susan dies on March 13.

1920 The Nineteenth Amendment to the U.S. Constitution is passed, giving women the right to vote.

BIBLIOGRAPHY

Barry, Kathleen. *Susan B. Anthony, A Biography*. Bloomington, IN: 1st Books Library, The International Online Library, 2000.

Burns, Ken, and Geoffrey Ward. *Not for Ourselves Alone: The Story of Elizabeth Cady Stanton and Susan B. Anthony*. New York: Alfred A. Knopf, 1999.

Sherr, Lynn. *Failure Is Impossible: Susan B. Anthony in Her Own Words*. New York: Times Books, a division of Random House, Inc., 1995.

SOURCE NOTES

All quotations are from *Susan B. Anthony, A Biography* by Kathleen Barry.

"it would never do . . . in the mill.": p. 16

"We did better . . . either could alone.": p. 70

"listen and learn": p. 71

"the new true woman": pp. 94, 105, 117, 129

"I am . . . to row upstream.": p. 116

"I never felt . . . Think of it!": p. 275

"Failure is impossible.": p. 381